summersdale

A LITTLE BIT OF WICKET WIT

Summersdale Publishers Ltd
46 West Street
Chichester
West Sussex
PO19 1RP
UK

www.summersdale.com

Printed and bound in Great Britain

ISBN: 978-1-84953-090-3

Disclaimer
Every effort has been made to attribute the quotations in this collection to the correct source. Should there be any omissions or errors in this respect we apologise and shall be pleased to make the appropriate acknowledgements in any future edition.

Substantial discounts on bulk quantities of Summersdale books are available to corporations, professional associations and other organisations. For details contact Summersdale Publishers by telephone: +44 (0) 1243 771107, fax: +44 (0) 1243 786300 or email: nicky@summersdale.com.

A LITTLE BIT OF
Wicket Wit

TOM HAY

Contents

Editor's Note

HRH The Duke of Edinburgh once scoffed at the 'widely held and quite erroneous belief that cricket is just another game'. This eclectic compendium, for its part, aptly disproves such misconceptions, showing how the gentleman's game has inspired both profound insights and some outrageously funny off-the-cuff humour.

The delightful mix of run-out rebuttals, wicket wisecracks and 'howzat' humiliations in this side-splitting book will ensure you will never be stumped for a witty return again.

A HEAVENLY GAME

I am confident they play
cricket in heaven. Wouldn't be
heaven otherwise, would it?

Patrick Moore

Cricket – it's more than a game. It's an institution.

Thomas Hughes, *Tom Brown's Schooldays*

Watching cricket has given
me more happiness than any
other activity in which I
have engaged.

A. A. Milne

In my opinion cricket is
too great a game to think
about statistically.

E. H. Hendren

Cricket is indescribable. How do you describe an orgasm?

Greg Matthews

Yesterday at The Oval had to be the most thrilling moment of my life… perhaps after the birth of my children.

Gladstone Small

Capital gain – smart sport –
fine exercise – very.

Charles Dickens on cricket, *The Pickwick Papers*

The love of cricket nowadays seems to be confined to those who watch it or read about it.

Arthur Mailey

—◆—

If I knew I was going to die today, I'd still want to hear the cricket scores.

J. H. Hardy

—◆—

GOING BATTY

When I'm batting, I like to pretend I'm a West Indian.

Darren Gough

I couldn't bat for the length of time required to score 500. I'd get bored and fall over.

Denis Compton

David Gower makes batting
look as easy as drinking tea.
Sir Leonard Hutton

It's like Manchester United
getting a penalty and Bryan
Robson taking it with
his head.

David Lloyd on the reverse sweep

———

They came to see me bat,
not to see you bowl.

**W. G. Grace on refusing to leave
the crease having been bowled
out by the first ball**

———

... my immediate objective was to hit the ball to each of the four corners of the field. After that, I tried not to be repetitive.

Lord Learie Constantine

It's hard work making batting
look effortless.

David Gower

BOWLED OVER

I don't want to do the
batsman any permanent
injury, just to cause him
concern – to hurt him a bit.

Dennis Lillee

There's nothing wrong with being aggressive – the bloke down the other end has a bat, some pads and a helmet.

Simon Jones

To be a great fast bowler,
you need a big heart and
a big bottom.

Fred Trueman

Though essentially good-natured, he had that vital weapon in the fast bowler's armoury: grumpiness.

Simon Hughes on Angus Fraser, *A Lot of Hard Yakka*

England will win if Camilla
Parker bowls.

Australian fans' banner

His bowling is like shooting down F-16s with sling shots. Even if they hit, no damage would be done.

Colin Croft on Angus Fraser in the Guyana Test

I won't miss bowling 20 overs
uphill into the wind.

Ian Botham

COACHES AND CAPTAINS

Pray God no professional may ever captain England.

Lord Hawke

Have nothing to do with coaches. In fact, if you should see one coming, go and hide behind the pavilion.

Bill O'Reilly

A man trying to get
your legs close together
when other men had spent a
lifetime trying to get
them wider apart.

**Rachael Heyhoe-Flint on the role
of the professional cricket coach**

I was never coached. I was
never told how to hold a bat.

Sir Donald Bradman

If I had my way, I would take
him to Traitor's Gate and
personally hang, draw
and quarter him.

Ian Botham on Ray Illingworth

Captaincy is 90 per cent luck
and ten per cent skill.
But don't try it without
that ten per cent.

Richie Benaud

Playing against a team
with Ian Chappell as captain
turns a cricket match into
gang warfare.

Mike Brearley

Amateurs have always
made, and always will make,
the best captains, and this
is only natural.

Allan Gibson Steel

You'll have the most miserable
time of your life.

**Brian Close to Ian Botham
on captaincy**

COME AGAIN?

On the first day, Logie
decided to chance his arm
and it came off.

Trevor Bailey

The Queen's Park Oval,
exactly as the name suggests,
absolutely round.

Tony Crozier

It's been a very slow and dull day, but it hasn't been boring. It's been a good, entertaining day's cricket.

Tony Benneworth

England have nothing
to lose here, apart from
this Test match.

David Lloyd

Yorkshire all out 232, Hutton
ill – I'm sorry, Hutton 111.

John Snagge

It is extremely cold here.
The England fielders are
keeping their hands in pockets
between balls.

Christopher Martin-Jenkins

His throw went absolutely
nowhere near where it
was going.

Richie Benaud

Matthew Fleming used to
be in the Green Jackets, but
the way he's batting suggests
he'd be better suited in the
Light Brigade.

Charles Colville

❥

Strangely, in slow-motion
replay, the ball seemed to
hang in the air for even longer.

David Acfield

❥

A very small crowd here today.
I can count the people on
one hand. Can't be more
than 30.

Michael Abrahamson

We didn't have any
metaphors in my day. We
didn't beat about the bush.

Fred Trueman

OFF THE RECORD

Cricket is full of theorists
who can ruin your game
in no time.

Ian Botham

If there is a game that attracts the half-baked theorists more than cricket, I have yet to hear of it.

Fred Trueman

They smile and then
they stab.

Geoff Boycott on cricket theorists

Generally, the people out
on the pitch are the ones
who know how to play the
game, not the ones who
are writing about it.

Marcus Trescothick

I will never be accepted by
the snob press.

Ray Illingworth

Mark Waugh's a great friend
of mine and he's got to make
a few quid somehow, even
by joining you blokes.

**Shane Warne speaking to
the press**

The media make mountains
from molehills to satisfy
producers and editors alike.

Mark Nicholas

Newspapers are only good
enough for wrapping up
fish and chips.

Martin Crowe

You have to try to reply to criticism with your intellect, not your ego.

Mike Brearley on handling the media

THE BATSMAN WORE WHITE

If you can't always play like a cricketer, you can at least look like one.

Sir Donald Bradman

Cricket needs umpires… with sartorial sharpness, instead of resembling a pair of Balkan refugees clad by Oxfam.

John Sheppard

I look like I do on the field
because what I do
is knackering.

Angus Fraser

Capable of looking more dishevelled at the start of a six-hour century than at the end of it.

Martin Johnson on Michael Atherton

The days of women's cricket
being seen as a knicker parade
must be over.

Norma Izard

You will sometimes see
a whole fielding team
resembling a herd of
cows at pasture.

**R. C. Robertson-Glasgow on the
habit of cricketers chewing gum**

It requires one to assume such
indecent postures.

Oscar Wilde on cricket

If they want me to get down to twelve stone, I would have to cut off a leg.

Ian Blackwell on the England selectors' orders for him to lose weight

COOL CRICKETERS

Concentration is sometimes
mistaken for grumpiness.
Michael Atherton

Difficult to be more laid
back without being actually
comatose.

Frances Edmonds on David Gower

It's like watching a swan.
What you see on the surface
bears no relation to the
activity going on underneath.

**David Gower on being accused of
being too laid back**

If something is not done to excess, it's hardly worth doing.

Peter Roebuck commenting on Ian Botham's character

[He's got a] reputation for
being awkward and arrogant,
probably because he is
awkward and arrogant.

**Frances Edmonds on her
husband Phil**

❖

Eeyore without the
joie de vivre.

Mike Selvey on Angus Fraser

❖

His personality was such
that it is remembered by
those who played with him
to the exclusion of his actual
performance.

John Arlott on W. G. Grace

I regret that my mouth
overtakes my brain.

Dermot Reeve

❦

He had all the loveable
qualities of a demented
rhinoceros.
Colin McCool on Bill O'Reilly

❦

COMPLETELY STUMPED

Sometimes, people think it's like
polo, played on horseback…
one guy thought it was a game
involving insects.

Clayton Lambert

Cricket is basically baseball
on Valium.

Robin Williams

Generally regarded as an incomprehensibly dull and pointless game.

Douglas Adams on cricket, *Life, the Universe and Everything*

Basically it's just a whole
bunch of blokes standing
around scratching themselves.

Kathy Lette

It's a silly game that
nobody wins.

Thomas Fuller

Personally, I have always
looked on cricket as
organised loafing.

William Temple

There is no more amateurish
professional game in the
world than cricket.

John Emburey

Cricket? It's rubbish.

Juninho

I would rather watch a
man at his toilet than
on a cricket field.

Robert Morley

We don't play this
game for fun.

Wilfred Rhodes

Cricket is the only game
where you can actually put
on weight while playing.
Tommy Docherty

DOWN IN ONE

Women are for batsmen, beer
is for bowlers. God help the
all-rounders.

Fred Trueman

Nothing yet devised by man
is worse for a sick hangover
than a day's cricket in
the summer sun.

Michael Parkinson

To see some of them sink
their drink is to witness
performances as awe-inspiring
as ever any of them displayed
on the cricket field.

Ian Botham

Let players drink at the beginning of the game, not after. It always works in our picnic matches.

Paul Hogan on how to brighten up cricket

I find it beautiful to watch and
I like that they break for tea.
That is very cool.

Jim Jarmusch

I don't think I've actually
drunk a beer for 15 years,
except a few Guinnesses in
Dublin, where it's the law.

Ian Botham

SEX OVER THE CENTURIES

Cricket is like sex films. They relieve frustration and tension.

Linda Lovelace

I suppose doing a love scene with Raquel Welch roughly corresponds to scoring a century before lunch.

Oliver Reed

I've never got to the
bottom of streaking.

Jonathan Agnew

Imran Khan has bodyguards outside his room, warding women off. I have guys warding them in.

Zia Mahmood

Women find it more than difficult not to cross and uncross their legs under his gaze.

Lord Tim Hudson on the sex appeal of Ian Botham

I tend to believe that cricket
is the greatest thing that
God ever created on earth…
although sex isn't too
bad either.

Harold Pinter

THE LIFE OF BRIAN

The bowler's Holding, the
batsman's Willey.

Brian Johnston

This bowler's like my dog:
three short legs and balls that
swing each way.

Brian Johnston

Welcome to Worcester where
we have just seen Barry
Richards hit one of Basil
D'Oliveira's balls clean out
of the ground.

Brian Johnston

Neil Harvey's at slip, with
his legs wide apart, waiting
for a tickle.

Brian Johnston

Turner looks a bit shaky and unsteady, but I think he's going to bat on – one ball left.

Brian Johnston

Fred Titmus has two short legs, one of them square.

Brian Johnston

❧

Welcome to Leicester, where
the captain Ray Illingworth
has just relieved himself at
the Pavilion End.

Brian Johnston

❧

ATTACKING SHOTS

Let's be getting at them
before they get at us.

W. G. Grace

Stuff that stiff upper lip crap.
Let's see how stiff it is when
it's split.

Jeff Thompson

He crossed the line between
eccentricity and idiocy far
too often for someone who
was supposed to be running
English cricket.

Ian Botham on Ted Dexter

A cricketer – a creature very
nearly as stupid as a dog.

Bernard Levin

So how're your wife
and my kids?

Rod Marsh to Ian Botham

Alan Green, the occasional off-spinner, might just turn a spin-drier but not much else.

Mihir Bose

Merv Hughes.

**Steve Waugh on being asked to
name his favourite animal**

❧

The MCC should change their name to the MCP.

Diana Edulji calling the MCC male chauvinist pigs after being refused entry to the Lord's pavilion

❧

Bloody medieval
most of them.

**Ian Botham on the English
cricket administration**

If someone wore a chocolate
bar on his head, Goughie
would follow suit.

Steve Oldham on Darren Gough

AN ENGLISHMAN'S GAME

It is more than a game, this cricket; it somehow holds up a mirror to English society.

Neville Cardus

Many Continentals think life is a game; the English think cricket is a game.

George Mikes

It is simply a social
necessity in England.

P. G. Wodehouse on cricket,
Piccadilly Jim

In an England cricket 11, the
flesh may be of the south, but
the bone is of the north and
the backbone is Yorkshire.

Sir Leonard Hutton

Our cricket is too gentle –
all of it.

Alec Stewart

John Henry Newman was as
English as roast beef, even if
he lacked a passion for cricket.

Clifford Longley

Distrusting the arts, the
English found a substitute in
cricket – a timeless blend of
formal dancing, rhetoric and
comic opera.

Kenneth Gregory,
Cricket's Last Romantic

THE HOUSE OF 'LORDS'

If you made him prime
minister tomorrow, he'd pick
this country up in ten minutes.

Billy Alley on Ian Botham

If Botham is an English folk hero, then this must be an alarming time for the nation.

David Miller

Cricket can be a bridge and
a glue… Cricket for peace
is my mission.

Muhammad Zia-ul-Haq

❦

I know why he's bought a
house by the sea… so he'll be
able to go for a walk on water.

**Fred Trueman on Geoff Boycott's
move to Poole Harbour**

❦

Say that cricket has nothing
to do with politics and you say
that cricket has nothing to
do with life.

John Arlott

Cricket, like the upper classes
and standards in general, is in
permanent decline.

Alan Ross

HOWZAT?

What a magnificent shot!
No, he's out.

Tony Greig

❖

If it had been a cheese roll,
it would never have got
past him.

**Graham Gooch on Mike Gatting
being bowled out in the 1993 Old
Trafford Test**

❖

❧

I can't bat, can't bowl and can't field these days. I've every chance of being picked for England.

Ray East

❧

Only two problems with
our team: brewer's droop
and financial cramp. Apart
from that we ain't bloody
good enough.

Charlie Parker

I can't really say I'm batting badly. I'm not batting long enough to be batting badly.

Greg Chappell

You should play every game as if it's your last, but make sure you perform well enough to ensure that it's not.

John Emburey

Nobody's perfect. You know what happened to the last man who was – they crucified him.

Geoff Boycott

A natural mistimer of the ball.

**Angus Fraser on Michael
Atherton**

Bowl better and bat better.

**Ricky Ponting on how Australia
can improve their performance**

THE WINNER TAKES IT ALL

I want to play cricket, it doesn't seem to matter if you win or lose.

Meat Loaf

Cricket is the only game I can enjoy without taking sides.

A. A. Milne

Some of them are quite nice
people, even though they
don't win as often as we do.

**Rachael Heyhoe-Flint on male
cricketers**

The game you are frightened
of losing is not worth winning.

Benny Green

The aim of English Test
cricket is, in fact, mainly
to beat Australia.

Jim Laker

I always played to win.

Hansie Cronje

❧

You are only as good as
your last game.

Ian Botham

❧

Any time the West Indies
lose, I cry.

Lance Gibbs

❧

But after all, it's not the
winning that matters, is it?

Alastair Cooke

❧

FROM ASHES TO ASHES

Endless cricket, like endless
anything else, simply grinds
you down.

Ted Dexter

I suppose it was like John Major running away from his circus background to be an accountant.

John Carr on leaving Middlesex for Barclay's bank

It's not in support of cricket
but as an earnest protest
against golf.

**Max Beerbohm when asked
to contribute to W. G. Grace's
testimonial**

✦

Ask me that again when
you're all in Dhaka and I'm
in Rome, watching Chelsea
playing Lazio!

**Alec Stewart on being asked if
he would regret retiring**

✦

I've had about ten operations.
I'm a bit like a battered old
Escort. You might find one
panel left that's an original.

Ian Botham

WICKET PHILOSOPHY

The English are not very
spiritual people, so they
invented cricket to give them
some idea of eternity.

George Bernard Shaw

The god of cricket likes
good manners.

George Lyttelton

Ninety per cent of cricket is
played in the mind.

Sir Richard Hadlee

Cricket: A game invented by religious fundamentalists to explain the idea of eternal hell to non-Christian indigenous peoples…

Joseph O'Connor

All is vanity, but cricket.

Rev. John Mitford

What do they know of cricket
who only cricket know?

C. L. R. James

What is human life but a
game of cricket?

Third Duke of Dorset

Have you enjoyed this book? If so,
why not write a review on your
favourite website?

Thanks very much for buying this
Summersdale book.

www.summersdale.com